The Best of

Sheikh Chilli

Compiled by Mrs. Rungeen Singh

Young Learner Publications
G-1A, Rattan Jyoti,
18 Rajendra Place,
New Delhi -110008 (INDIA)
Ph.: 25750801, 25820556, 25755559
Fax: 91-11-25764396

Printed at : Kumar Offset Printers, Delhi-110092

CONTENTS

SHEIKH ON A TRAIN

Sheikh Chilli was four years old when he sat in a train for the first time with his father and mother.

Train tickets were not required for children below three years. Sheikh was four years old but Sheikh's father did not buy a ticket for Sheikh because he wanted to save money. He bought only two tickets, one for himself and the other for his wife.

The train was on its way when the ticket checker came to check their tickets.

After checking his parents tickets, the ticket checker asked for Sheikh's train ticket.

His father said, "My son does not need a ticket as he is only three years old."

"I don't think he is three years old. He looks much older," remarked the checker.

"Is he your son or mine?" asked the father angrily.

"Yours, thank God! But he looks so big!" exclaimed the checker.

"What can I do about his size? I am telling you, he is three years old," insisted his father.

Sheikh wanted to say something, but his father glared at him daring him to say anything.

"You tell me, child. How old are you?" asked the checker looking at Sheikh.

Then Sheikh spoke up, "At home I am four years old but in the train I am three years old."

"What are you saying? Keep quiet," shouted Sheikh's father.

Sheikh asked, "Why are you telling lies, father? You know I am four years old."

The ticket checker pointed out to the father, "See. I was right. You were telling a lie."

The father was caught on the wrong foot so he said, "I am sorry."

The ticket checker said, "I should take a huge fine from you, but I will not take it because your son is so honest. But make sure never to do this again."

The father answered, "How nice of you! Now I will never travel by train without a ticket for Sheikh. Today my son has taught me a lesson that we should always be honest."

TWO YARDS OF MILK

After a few years, his father died and Sheikh Chilli lived alone with his mother.

Sheikh was a very stupid boy but his mother had to send him to buy things from the market because there was no one else to help her.

One day his mother told Sheikh to go to the market and buy milk for one anna.

When he reached the shop, he saw that the shopkeeper had two pots, one in each hand. While pouring the hot milk from one pot to another, he would stretch one hand away from the other.

The milk then looked like a long, white cloth between the two pots.

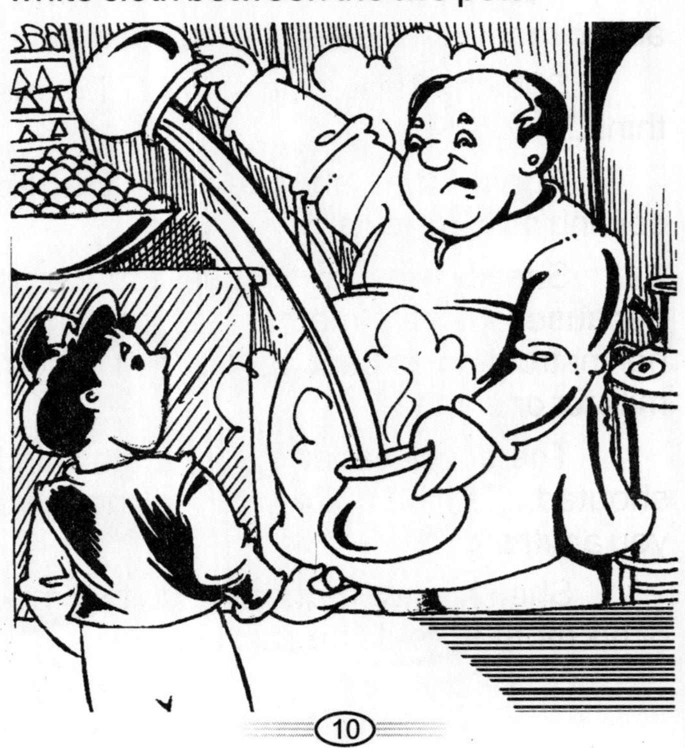

Sheikh Chilli was really surprised to see this because he did not know that the shopkeeper was doing this to cool the milk. Actually Sheikh thought that the shopkeeper was measuring the milk in this way.

The shopkeeper asked him, "What do you want?"

"I want to buy milk," said Sheikh.

"How much milk do you want?" asked the shopkeeper.

Sheikh Chilli said, "Wait, let me think."

Again the shopkeeper started cooling milk in the same manner.

Sheikh was at a loss for words because Sheikh's mother had given him no instruction except telling him to get milk for one anna.

The shopkeeper grew irritated and shouted, "Tell me quickly or I will not give you anything."

Sheikh knew that he had to buy milk or his mother would be angry.

He thought, "Money is counted as rupees, annas and paisa but this shopkeeper seems to be measuring the milk in yards, feet and inches. And mother has asked me to get milk for one anna. What should I do?"

He thought some more and then he said loudly, "Give me two yards of milk."

Everyone burst out laughing at Sheikh's foolishness.

WHERE DID THE OIL GO?

One day Sheikh Chilli was flying a kite when his mother called him and asked him to get mustard oil worth eight annas from the market.

His mother also gave him a big tumbler for the oil and told Sheikh to be careful in bringing the oil.

Sheikh Chilli went to the shop and asked for eight annas worth of mustard oil from the shopkeeper.

The shopkeeper filled the tumbler and then said, “I have given seven annas worth of oil. One anna worth of oil is still left. In which utensil should I give it to you?”

Sheikh thought for a long time and then his hand felt the hollow bottom of the tumbler and he got the idea that the hollow of the container would be enough to hold one anna worth of oil.

He turned the full tumbler upside down and told the shocked shopkeeper to fill the one anna worth of oil in the hollow at the bottom of the tumbler.

The shopkeeper was too surprised to say anything. He put the one anna worth of oil in the hollow of the tumbler.

Sheikh carried the tumbler home very carefully. His mother asked, "Sheikh, where is the rest of the oil?"

Sheikh turned the tumbler upside down again and replied, "Here mother."

She exclaimed, "But there is nothing here in the tumbler and you have spilt what little oil you had brought!"

"But I saw the shopkeeper put the oil in the tumbler," insisted Sheikh.

"Do you know what you have done son? You have thrown all the oil down. You have wasted all the eight annas and also your time," explained his mother.

Sheikh looked at the tumbler and remarked, "But the shopkeeper had given me mustard oil in this tumbler. What happened to it? Where did it go?"

Just then the shopkeeper's son came and said to Sheikh's mother, "Father has sent this seven annas worth of mustard oil because when Sheikh had turned over the tumbler in the shop, the oil had dropped into the oil tin itself."

Sheikh's mother took the oil and thanked the boy, but Sheikh still stood looking at the tumbler in a daze.

He wondered again, "I saw the shopkeeper pour oil in this tumbler. Where did it go?"

THE SLEEPING UMBRELLA!

One evening Sheikh Chilli's mother was happy because she had earned more money than usual. So she bought a lot of food stuff and made a wonderful dinner. Sheikh ate to his heart's content and felt sleepy.

But his mother remarked, "First go and give this dish to our neighbour or she might go to sleep."

It was raining outside and Sheikh requested his mother, "Please give me an umbrella."

His mother gave an umbrella to Sheikh. He took the dish, went out and gave it to their neighbour.

He came back soon. The umbrella was wet and his mother advised, "Keep the umbrella in a corner of your room and you go to bed. Go quickly child or you will get sick."

Sheikh yawned sleepily and went to his room.

Next morning, his mother came to wake up Sheikh.

She was amazed when she saw that the wet umbrella was lying on the bed and Sheikh was standing in the corner of the room, sleeping.

"Wake up, Sheikhu. What are you doing in the corner of your room?" asked the mother.

"You only told me to put myself in the corner of my room. But Mother, I am very weary. It is so tiring to stand and sleep," answered Sheikh.

The mother exclaimed, "Oh, you fool! I never said this. I told you to put the umbrella in the corner of your room. Not only have you suffered all night, but the wet umbrella has also wet your bed."

Sheikh was so tired because he had been standing up the whole night that he dropped down on the floor and went to sleep.

His mother quickly removed the wet sheets and made Sheikh lie down on the bed. Then Sheikh slept peacefully for a very long time.

His mother wondered, "Why is my son so forgetful and stupid? If only he could become clever!"

I AM 'HUSSAIN'

One day a man came to Sheikh and asked, "Are you Hussain?"

Now Sheikh Chilli was tired of being called stupid by one and all, so he decided to act smart!

He looked at the man and said, "Yes, I am Hussain."

The man complained, “Last month I bought a goat from you. That goat has run away.”

Sheikh just smiled.

The man went on, “The goat must have come back to you.”

Sheikh chuckled and said, “Yes.”

The man demanded, “You must give the goat or my money back to me.”

Sheikh giggled more. The man thought that Sheikh was teasing him and feeling irritated, he started hitting Sheikh. Many people crowded around them.

Everyone was surprised because Sheikh went on grinning, even though he was being beaten so badly.

For some time the man kept hitting Sheikh and Sheikh started laughing heartily. This made the man angrier.

He started kicking Sheikh so hard that blood came out from Sheikh’s mouth, but Sheikh kept on laughing.

Finally the man got tired of beating Sheikh and went away.

Then Sheikh boasted to the people, "See I am so clever. I fooled that man."

"How did you fool him? You were the one being beaten," gasped the people standing there.

"Yes and that was because I let him think that I am Hussain when I am not. See how I fooled that man?" grinned Sheikh Chilli.

Everyone was shocked at Sheikh's extreme stupidity.

PRAY AND GET A BUFFALO

A holy man came to Sheikh's village to preach the people to pray to God several times everyday.

He told them, "If you all pray regularly, then God will give you a buffalo as a reward."

Sheikh really wanted a buffalo. He had often dreamt that if he had a buffalo, he would become rich. But Sheikh did not want to be fooled.

He thought and thought.

Finally Sheikh said to the holy man, "There must be some trick in this. What if we don't get a buffalo?"

The holy man replied, "God is great. Try it out."

From that day Sheikh became very regular in saying his prayers. He said his prayers many times a day sometimes even skipping his meals, surprising everyone for everyone knew that he was fond of eating.

After a month he waited outside his house for a buffalo. When the buffalo did not come, Sheikh went to the holy man to ask him about the buffalo.

"I didn't get a buffalo though I prayed. Tell God to give me a buffalo," said Sheikh.

The holy man said, "God can't give you a buffalo. You have to buy it."

Sheikh said, "You told us that we would get a buffalo. I have prayed regularly, I must get one."

The holy man said, "I had said that you will get a buffalo just to make you pray to the Almighty."

"So it was a trick," shouted Sheikh.

The holy man replied, "This was not a trick. It was just a way to make you pray."

Sheikh shouted, "It was a trick. Do you think I am stupid? I understood everything, so I have been clever too."

"How?" asked the holy man.

Sheikh answered, "I did not pray. I just moved my lips. See I fooled everyone. Ha! Ha! Ha! See how clever I am!"

PYJAMAS IN THE WELL

One morning, Sheikh's mother washed Sheikh's clothes and hung them to dry on the clothesline on the terrace.

After sometime a violent storm came. A very strong wind began to blow and there was a lot of dust everywhere.

Sheikh's mother shut all the doors and windows of her house.

Then she remembered that the washed clothes were upstairs, but she could not go out in the storm as it was very strong.

As soon as the storm stopped, the mother went upstairs to look for the washed clothes.

Unfortunately, all the washed clothes were lying strewn around in the mud.

She picked them up and came down and told Sheikh, "I am glad that I have found all the clothes, but I am unhappy that your pyjamas have fallen into the well."

Sheikh said, "Mother, why are you unhappy? You should be happy."

"Why?" asked his mother, surprised at what he was saying.

Sheikh replied, “See the positive side. What if I had been wearing the pyjamas? Then I too would have been inside the well but I am safe. So you should be happy to have such a wonderful son like me alive and kicking.”

“If only you were so wonderful Sheikhu,” sighed the mother.

EGG OR MANGO?

Sheikh Chilli was walking back home when he saw Babban coming with something in his hand. Sheikh felt very curious to know what Babban was holding in his hand.

He went to Babban and asked, "What do you have in your hand?"

As usual Babban wanted to tease Sheikh Chilli, so he hid the egg he had in his hand behind his back.

He replied, "You are so wise Sheikh. Why don't you tell me what I have in my hand?"

Sheikh felt very proud of himself and said, "Then ask me, Babban."

Babban repeated question, "Ok Sheikh. Can you tell me what is in my hand?"

Sheikh thought for some time and then shrugged saying, "My brain is not working. Give me some hints. Only then can I guess."

Babban said, "It has a yellow yolk in the centre. It has white jelly outside the yolk and is covered with a white shell."

Sheikh thought for a long time but in vain. It was very difficult for him.

Then suddenly Sheikh looked at Babban with his eyes shining brightly and smiled, “I have got the answer. It is simple.”

“Tell me,” said Babban.

“What you have in your hand is a mango in the middle. Right, isn’t it?” enquired Sheikh eagerly.

“What else?” asked Babban.

“The mango has curd all around it,” said Sheikh.

“Aha! Very good thinking. What else?” muttered Babban, now really amused.

“The curd is kept in a pot which is painted white,” described Sheikh further.

Babban laughed, “How clever of you Sheikh. No one else could have answered this.”

Babban walked away thinking why the stupid Sheikh was not able to understand that he had an ordinary egg in his hand. He laughed for a very long time at Sheikh’s stupidity.

On the other hand Sheikh Chilli also laughed for a long time thinking why the stupid Babban had put a mango in curd in a white painted pot, "What would he do with it? Silly fellow!"

His mother said, "Sheikhu, go to the tailor. You must not look here and there but walk straight to his shop."

"How do I reach the tailor shop?" asked Sheikh.

His mother answered, "Just go down the main road, look straight and you will reach the shop of the tailor."

Sheikh started walking. He looked straight and walked on. He did not look here or there.

Then he thought, "Why is it taking me so long to reach the tailor's shop?"

All of a sudden he banged into a tree and hurt his nose. He rubbed his aching nose.

"How did this tree come in the middle of the road?" thought Sheikh.

Then he looked around. He was not on a road. He was in a field and there was no road in sight.

"How did the road reach here? My feet are to blame. They brought me here," thought Sheikh.

He stomped his feet angrily but that did not help. Then he climbed a tree to look for the road.

He looked in all directions and saw the road on the other side of the tree at some distance.

He thought of jumping down to get to the road. He caught a branch and was hanging on it, about to jump, when he looked down.

There was a well just under him. The water in the well shone in the sunlight. Sheikh felt very nice. He felt like a kite flying in the air. He started dreaming.

He was a king and was sitting on the elephant alongwith his mother, wearing beautiful clothes. Oh! How happy he felt.

Clipetty clop. Clipetty clop.

"But that is not the sound of a running elephant. It is more like the sound of a running horse," thought Sheikh.

He opened his eyes and saw a soldier on a horse, coming towards him galloping very fast.

The soldier was shouting loudly, "Boy don't worry. I will save you. I will jump over the well. You leave the branch and I will hold you from your waist and carry you to safety."

The soldier made his horse jump over the well. He caught Sheikh's hands.

But alas! Sheikh did not leave the branch. Now they both hung over the well.

"You stupid fool. Why didn't you leave the branch?" asked the soldier.

Sheikh said, “I am sorry but I don't know why I did not leave the branch. I could have left the branch like this.”

Sheikh then left the branch and as the soldier was holding Sheikh's feet, both of them fell down into the well.

“You are really stupid,” shouted the soldier angrily.

“But you are clean now. Till now I could not see your face because you were covered with dust. Now the water of the well has cleaned you,” said Sheikh happily.

“Why are you staring at me?” asked the soldier.

“I love your moustache. It is straight and then it hangs down on the sides,” said Sheikh.

“No, at the ends, my moustache curls up into a circle. Just now it is hanging on the sides because it is wet. Now stop talking about my moustache. Let me think of a way to get out of this well?” said the soldier.

"Why do you want to get out of the well? I don't want to get out. I am having fun here," smiled Sheikh pointing at the soldier's wet moustache again.

"But I am not having fun," snapped the angry soldier. He started calling out loudly, "Help! Help!"

Sheikh said, "Please shout again. It is so nice to see your moustache wobbling with your words."

The soldier screamed angrily, "Eeee. Will you stop it? Here I am in a hurry to get out of the well and you are talking about my moustache all the time."

Sheikh kept quiet when the soldier called for help again. Then they heard some shouts.

The soldier shouted back, "Come here. We are in the well. Save us. Help! Help!"

After sometime some farmers came to the well. They had heard the soldier shouting and had come to help.

The farmers looked around and after a while they brought two ropes to take out the soldier and Sheikh from the well. They lowered the ropes into the well and held the other ends.

The soldier and Sheikh caught the ropes and they climbed out of the well. The soldier thanked the farmers.

As the soldier started to walk to his house, Sheikh chuckled, "Soldier, your moustache has started curling." That was too much for the soldier.

Angrily, the soldier ran after Sheikh shouting, "Moustache! Moustache! Will you stop talking about it? You are such a pest. I will beat you."

Scared, Sheikh ran away from there and the soldier then rode away on his horse.

Sheikh reached his house and his mother enquired, "Sheikhu, how did you get so wet and muddy?"

"I fell into a well from a tree," replied Sheikh.

"Well? How did you reach a well? I sent you to the tailor. There is no well on the way. I cannot trust you to do even a small thing. Where have you been?" asked his mother.

"I enjoyed an adventure and I have decided to grow the longest moustache in the world when I grow up," said Sheikh.

He placed her hair on his upper lip as a moustache.

"Moustache? Oh Sheikhu! Again you have been day dreaming," muttered the poor mother, totally mystified by Sheikh's story.

SICKLE FEVER

"Sheikhu, today I am going to a wedding to help with the work," said his mother.

"Mother, last time you got wonderful sweets. What will you get this time?" asked Sheikh enthusiastically.

"I don't know but I will be given something nice to eat as well as some extra money," replied his mother.

Sheikh loved to eat. He started dreaming about the wonderful sweets he would get to eat in the evening.

"Sheikhu. Are you listening to me?" he heard his mother say.

"Yes, mother," said Sheikh.

"You must go and cut some grass from the nearby forest. Here is a sickle. Don't lose it," warned his mother.

"Oh Mother! Why must I work? I don't like to work. I only want to sit and enjoy myself."

"My friend has said that she will give you money if you cut grass for her cow and I will not give you sweets if you don't cut the grass," said his mother to Sheikh.

Sheikh did not want to miss the sweets that he would get in the evening, so he went to cut the grass.

For the first time he was careful in doing his work. He cut the grass, then he tied the grass and gave the bundle of grass to his mother's friend.

She gave him two annas for it and Sheikh ran home happily. Suddenly he remembered that he had left the sickle in the forest.

He knew that his mother would be angry if he lost the sickle, so he ran to get it from the forest.

Sheikh found the sickle and he bent to pick it up. Then he screamed, "Aaaaaaah!" as he touched the hot blade of the sickle.

Sheikh felt that he had burnt his hand when he touched the sickle. He stood staring at the sickle for a very long time.

Just then Lallan from his village passed that way. Lallan enquired of Sheikh, "What are you doing?"

"Something has happened to the sickle. It has fever. It is very hot. Can you help me?" asked Sheikh.

"Yes. I know the cure. We will tie it and put it in the water of the well. Then the sickle will recover from its fever," advised Lallan.

They tied the sickle to a rope and dipped it in the water of the well.

Lallan knew that the sickle was burning because it had become hot in the sun, but he wanted to tease Sheikh.

He told Sheikh, "Let us leave the sickle here in the well. In the evening, you can come and take it home."

Sheikh walked home with Lallan who was all this while planning to steal the sickle.

He knew that if Sheikh lost the sickle then Sheikh would get a beating from his mother and that is what Lallan wanted. He always felt happy when Sheikh was punished.

Sheikh reached home and rested. He thought that he would bring the sickle from the well before his mother came.

So in the evening, he walked out of his house to get the sickle from the well.

On the way he passed Lallan's house. He heard someone groaning with pain.

He looked around and realised that the sound was coming from within the house.

Sheikh quickly ran inside the house and saw that Lallan's grandmother was lying on a cot. When he touched her, he realised that she had fever.

"Don't worry, Granny. I know the cure for fever," said Sheikh. He picked her up and took her outside.

"Where are you taking Granny?" asked another friend.

Sheikh said, "She has fever. I am taking her to cure her."

Sheikh walked away with Granny and after some time Lallan and his father returned to their house.

They had gone to get medicine for Granny, and now when they reached their house, they found that Granny was missing.

They began searching everywhere for her. The friend told Lallan that he had seen Sheikh carry Granny away to cure her of the fever.

Lallan at once understood where Sheikh would have taken his Granny. He ran towards the well.

He heaved a sigh of relief when he saw Granny with Sheikh near the well. He was glad to find his granny. Sheikh had untied the sickle and was tying Granny to the rope.

"What are you doing?" shouted Lallan.

"Oh Lallan! It is good that you have come because your Granny is very heavy," said Sheikh.

"What are you doing?" screamed Lallan's father.

"This is the best cure for fever, Uncle. My sickle got cured as Lallan had said. I have tied Granny with this rope. We will put her in the well," said Sheikh.

"Did Lallan tell you about this cure?" asked Lallan's father.

Sheikh replied, "Yes Uncle and my sickle has been cured of its fever."

Lallan's father said, "And now I will cure Lallan's fever." The father started beating Lallan who started crying.

Then his father ordered him, "Now help me pick up Granny. She would have died had we not come in time."

The weeping Lallan and his father picked up Granny and went home.

Sheikh picked up his sickle but he was very confused.

He thought, "Why didn't they put Granny into the well?" Why did Lallan's father beat Lallan though he had cured the sickle? Why did Lallan's father say that Granny could have died? When the water of the well can cure the fever of the sickle then it could surely relieve granny's fever too! People are so strange and so stupid."

SHEIKH CATCHES A THIEF

Sheikh's mother was helping her dear friend Fatima with the wedding preparations of her daughter.

When she returned from her friend's house, she brought sweets for Sheikh to eat.

After Sheikh had finished eating, she said, "My friend Fatima was giving me a watermelon but it was too heavy for me to carry. I have left it there. You can get it tomorrow."

"But what if someone eats it in the night?" asked the worried Sheikh.

"No one is there in the house. They have gone to another village for a feast," answered his mother.

Sheikh and his mother lay down to sleep, but Sheikh could only think of the watermelon.

When he saw that his mother had gone to sleep, he could not stop himself.

He got up and went out of his house, straight to the house of his mother's friend.

He then saw that the watermelon was kept on top of some sacks of coal, as his mother had told him. He quickly ran to pick up the watermelon. Just then he heard some voices.

"Who can they be?" thought Sheikh. His mother had said that there was no one in the house.

He ran and hid behind the sacks afraid that he might get caught. Then he saw Lallan and another man walk in.

Lallan said, “Oooohh!”

The other man with him got scared and gasped, “What was that sound?”

“Oh! My body is aching. Because of that Sheikh Chilli, my father beat me really hard,” groaned Lallan.

“Is that all? You scared me. I thought that someone had come,” whispered the other man.

“Let us be quick about it. This house is haunted. What if some ghost comes here?” said Lallan.

Then the other man opened a cupboard and took out a lot of jewellery. Sheikh was shocked.

This was the jewellery that Fatima had bought for her daughter’s wedding. His mother had told him about the jewellery.

The thief then gave some pieces of jewellery to Lallan and kept the rest in his bag.

Lallan said, “Give me more.”

The thief said, “I did all the work, so

this is enough for you. Take the watermelon if you want."

Lallan held the watermelon to lift it up but Sheikh had already caught it. Sheikh would not let go.

"Ghost! A ghost is holding this. Help! Help!" shouted Lallan.

Sheikh felt afraid and shouted too, "Help! Ghost!"

"Hush! Whose voice was that?" shouted Lallan."

Keep quiet or we will be caught," said the thief.

But the neighbours had already heard Lallan and Sheikh shouting for help.

They came running and Sheikh yelled quickly, "Catch them. They are thieves." The two thieves were caught with all the jewellery.

They all waited till Fatima came and she was given the jewellery.

Fatima counted the pieces of jewellery and saw that everything was intact. She thanked Sheikh who quickly picked up the watermelon.

Everyone praised Sheikh. The people carried Sheikh home on their shoulders as if he was a hero. His mother was very proud of him for once. She was so happy that she cut the watermelon at once for Sheikh to eat.

Sheikh felt very happy with himself and he finished the whole watermelon, relishing every bite of it.

I AM A 'MOUSE'

"Oh you cats, leave me! Don't chase me. Go away all of you," yelled Sheikh.

His mother had been sleeping. She woke up when she heard Sheikh shouting and screaming in his sleep.

She shouted, “Wake up, Sheikh. You have been dreaming.”

Sheikh woke up and said, “Many cats are after me.”

“There are no cats here Sheikhu. Did you dream again that you are a mouse?” she asked, feeling concerned for her son.

“Yes, Mother and all the cats of the village were after me. See I am still a mouse,” cried Sheikh.

“No, you are not a mouse. You are a boy. My poor child, don’t worry. I will take you to the doctor,” consoled his mother.

Next day, Sheikh’s mother took him to the doctor and told the doctor that Sheikh had started getting nightmares of cats chasing him.

The doctor asked some questions about his childhood and she said, “When Sheikh was a baby, a cat had scratched him badly. Do you think that could be the reason for these dreams?”

"Maybe, but don't worry. Let Sheikh take this medicine. Bring him to me every evening," said the doctor to Sheikh's mother.

As they were leaving, the doctor advised, “Sheikh, just try and remember that you are a boy and a very handsome boy.”

Sheikh became very happy on being praised and every evening he would go to the doctor.

The doctor would listen to him for an hour and the medicine he gave was just to help Sheikh get a good night’s sleep.

One day, as Sheikh came out after visiting the doctor, he saw a cat and feeling scared, he hid behind the doctor.

The doctor said, “The cat can do nothing to you. You are a boy who is bigger than the cat. You are not a mouse.”

Sheikh asked the doctor, “I know doctor, but has anyone told the cat?”

The doctor laughed and said, “A boy who can speak like this cannot be a mouse.”

After regular treatment, finally the bad dreams stopped and Sheikh stopped thinking that he was a mouse being chased by cats. His mother was a relieved person.

THE THUMB MARKS

Sheikh's mother now wanted Sheikh to get a job and earn some money.

She asked Sheikh's uncle to get him a job. With a friend's help, Sheikh's uncle got Sheikh a job in the King's court. Sheikh was very happy on meeting the King.

The King wanted to know the number of villages in his state and how many people were there in each village.

He wanted Sheikh to get the thumb marks of all the people so that they could be counted. He said that Sheikh would be paid one paisa for every thumb mark and that he should get atleast one hundred and fifty thumb marks.

The friend of the uncle told Sheikh, “I have heard that you are very stupid. Don’t spoil anything with your stupidity.”

Sheikh nodded and started working very hard. Satisfied, his uncle thought, “Sheikh will earn a lot of money now.”

Sheikh was in the villages for a long time. He worked very hard for the first time in his life.

When he finished his work, he went to the friend of the uncle. Sheikh showed him the thumbprints and was paid for them.

Then Sheikh went to his uncle and said, “Your friend thought that I am stupid, but I showed him that I am clever.”

"What have you done?" asked the uncle alarmed.

Sheikh laughed and boasted, " I got many thousands of thumb marks but I showed him just one hundred and fifty. The rest I threw away."

"What? Are you crazy, Sheikh?" exclaimed the Uncle."

"Why?" asked Sheikh, not understanding what his uncle was saying.

The uncle said, "By throwing away the thumb marks, you have lost a lot of money that you could have earned."

"How?" asked Sheikh Chilli. His stupid mind could not understand this.

The uncle said, "You would have got one paisa for each thumb mark. You got thousands of thumb marks."

"So what?" asked Sheikh.

"So you would have earned thousands of paise," said the Uncle.

"So what did I do wrong?" said Sheikh, still confused.

"You threw away all the papers with the thumb marks. You have lost all that money you would have got for the thumb marks," said his Uncle.

Sheikh couldn't understand this. The uncle knew that Sheikh Chilli would do foolish things throughout his life and create trouble for his family.

The uncle did not want to suffer because of Sheikh's stupidity.

The uncle then decided to send Sheikh back to his mother.

MAN IN THE GRAVEYARD

The foolishness of Sheikh Chilli had always troubled his mother. Now she wanted him to learn about life, the difficulties and become more worldly wise.

So when a relative died, she sent Sheikh to the funeral. It was the first time that Sheikh had seen a graveyard.

Next night, Sheikh was near the same graveyard on his way back from the village where he had gone for a feast.

Suddenly he heard the voice of a man yelling, "Help! Help!"

Sheikh strained his ears to find out where the voice was coming from. He looked above and around.

Then he saw a man who had fallen into a ditch by the side of the graveyard.

The man shouted, "Please take me out from here. It is very cold here."

Sheikh remembered, that earlier when he had come to the graveyard, the dead body had been buried under mud.

Now he said, “Of course I know why you are feeling cold. They forgot to put mud on you.”

Sheikh Chilli started throwing mud on the man in the ditch, while the man continued screaming that he was not dead, but alive.

THE DOCTOR'S EARS

One day, the doctor asked Sheikh, "What would happen if my ears fell off?"

Sheikh replied, "You would surely become deaf and blind too for there would be no ears to hold your spectacles!"

The doctor burst out laughing.

WHERE DOES THE ROAD GO?

One day, a man stopped Sheikh on the road and asked, "Where does this road go?"

Sheikh replied, "Nowhere! We can go on the road but the road does not go anywhere."

The man laughed and agreed, "Yes, you are right."

PUMPKIN EGGS

Sheikh Chilli was roaming around another village when he saw a field filled with pumpkins.

Sheikh did not recognise the pumpkins because he had never seen a pumpkin before.

He asked the farmer, "What are these things?"

The farmer wanted to have some fun, so he said, "These are special eggs of the earth."

Sheikh asked, "What comes out of these eggs?"

The farmer answered, "It could be baby animals of any type."

"I want to buy one. What is the cost? I have only these coins with me," said Sheikh.

The farmer took all his money and said, "You look clever, so I will give you one egg of the earth for this money."

"How will it hatch?" asked Sheikh.

"I will tell you," said the farmer. The pumpkin was too heavy to pick up, so the farmer left it on the ground.

The farmer made a platform on the tree with bamboo sticks and covered it with hay.

He told Sheikh to sit on the platform till the egg of the earth hatched.

Sheikh sat on the tree seat waiting for the egg to hatch.

The farmer would give him food to eat, but the farmer would also bring people from his village to see 'the idiot' Sheikh sitting on the tree seat.

On the third day, Sheikh was feeling very tired of reclining on the tree seat. He tried to sit up and then he fell on the pumpkin that was kept on the ground under the tree.

As he fell, the pumpkin burst open. A baby deer had been sleeping nearby.

When Sheikh fell down, the frightened baby deer ran from there. Sheikh saw it running away.

He thought that the egg had hatched and the baby deer had come out from the egg.

Sheikh Chilli ran after the baby deer but it ran away and Sheikh had to come back empty handed. He started crying.

He walked to the farmer who was watching Sheikh with his friends. All of them were laughing at Sheikh's stupidity.

"I lost the baby deer that came out of the egg," cried Sheikh.

The farmer consoled him, "You go home. If I see the baby deer, I will send it to you."

Sheikh went home crying, leaving the farmer and his friends laughing.

DOG IN THE HOLE

Sheikh Chilli was walking around aimlessly when he saw a hole as wide as a well.

He started thinking about the hole in the ground. He could not see inside the hole because of the dirty water. How deep was it?

This question troubled his mind again and again. Then he could not stop himself.

He thought, "I must find out how deep this hole is. Then people will take me to be a clever person."

He sat down and thought of some way to find it out.

When he could not think of a way, he looked around. There was nothing with which he could measure the depth.

Then he saw a log and an idea came to his mind. He felt very clever.

He started pulling the log towards the hole.

It was very heavy, still he pushed and pulled till he got the log near the hole.

Then he threw the log into the hole. Suddenly a dog ran in and dashed after the log.

Sheikh was shocked at the speed with which the dog had run after the log.

He could not think of a reason why a dog would run after a log. He tried to find an answer, but he couldn't.

Then a man came looking here and there as if searching for someone. He looked all around and saw Sheikh.

He asked Sheikh, "Have you seen a white dog?"

Sheikh nodded, "Yes. He just dashed into this hole."

The man said, "That is not possible because he was tied to a very heavy log."

"I threw the log into this hole," explained Sheikh.

"What! But why would you do such a thing?" asked the man.

"I wanted to see how deep the hole is," replied Sheikh.

"Do you know what you have done?" asked the man.

"Yes. I threw a log in the hole," repeated Sheikh.

"You idiot. You have killed my dog," shouted the man .

"But I didn't throw the dog in the hole," said Sheikh.

Angrily the man started beating Sheikh who still did not understand what wrong he had done.

THE RIGHT PRICE

Sheikh was flying a kite and enjoying every moment of it.

His mother called him and said, "Sheikh, there is no money in the house."

Sheikh asked, "So what should I do?"

His mother spoke on, "Go and sell this cock and get some money otherwise there will be nothing to eat in the evening."

These were words that Sheikh hated to hear. He did not like being hungry. So he agreed to go to the market to sell the cock.

His mother warned, "Don't sell the cock for less than two rupees. Try to get the right price, Sheikhu."

"Don't worry, Mother. I will manage," answered Sheikh confidently.

Sheikh went to the market and sat down with the cock. He wanted to make his mother happy by selling the cock for the right price.

A man came and asked, “I want to buy this cock. What is the cost?”

“I will sell it only for the right price,” replied Sheikh.

“I have spent all my money. I have just one rupee left,” said the man.

“Left? No. I want the right price,” insisted Sheikh.

The man went away. A cheat had been listening to Sheikh talking to the man.

He came to Sheikh and commented, “You are very clever. This man was trying to cheat you, but you didn’t let him.”

Sheikh agreed happily, “I can’t help it. I am clever.”

The cheat added, “You know what is right and what is left. Do you know the right price?”

Sheikh replied, “Of course! My mother said that I should sell it for not less than two.”

“But I will pay you more. I will give you four and I will give it with my right hand to make it the right price,” answered the cheat.

Sheikh looked at him blankly. All this was too much for his brain. He took the four annas that the cheat gave him.

Happy with the deal, the cheat took the cock and went away.

Sheikh went home and gave the four anna coins to his mother, but to his surprise she started crying.

"I know why you are crying. You are happy that I have sold the cock for such a lot of money," said Sheikh.

His mother shouted, "No, you fool. I am crying because you are stupid. I had told you to sell it for two rupees but you sold it for four annas."

"Four is more than two, Mother," answered Sheikh.

"Sheikhu. Sixteen annas make a rupee. You have sold the cock for four annas. It is a loss for us," cried his mother.

Sheikh asked, "What do you mean?"

"I mean that you have got less money than you should have got," explained his mother.

She started crying even more when Sheikh looked at her blankly and blamed her, saying, "Mother, you don't know your sums. Four is more than two."

His mother exclaimed, "Oh Lord! What do I do with this fool?"

TO SEE HIS IN LAWS

One day Sheikh Chilli was eating when his mother said, "Sheikhu. You know that your marriage was fixed when you were small."

"Uh!" smiled Sheikh shyly.

"The girl's parents have called you," said his mother. Sheikh blushed.

His mother continued smilingly, “Come on Sheikhu. Why are you shy? You are not the bride.”

Though she joked with him, his mother was worried about Sheikh. She knew that he was very stupid.

She was afraid that if the parents of the girl came to know that he was really stupid, then the marriage could be called off. But now Sheikh had to go to the girl’s house as they had invited him.

So she instructed him to act clever and mature in the girl’s house.

Then Sheikh left home and started his journey to the village where the girl and her parents lived.

On the way, he saw some juicy berries. His mouth began to water seeing the juicy berries, so he started eating them one after the other. He was so busy eating that he did not see that there were many ants in the bushes.

The ants crawled inside his clothes and started biting him. He felt very itchy.

Sheikh jumped up and down trying to scratch all over his body. Then he took off his clothes because he couldn't tolerate the itch any longer.

Suddenly he remembered that he had to reach his in-law's house, so he began to run.

On the way, he realised that he had forgotten to wear his clothes, but it was too late.

Some soldiers saw him and caught him. They asked him why he was without clothes.

Sheikh told them about the ants. The soldiers searched his bag and found that he had a fresh set of clothes with him. They asked him why had he not worn them.

Sheikh explained, "I was looking for a bush or tree, but couldn't find one. I am not so shameless as to dress in the open."

The soldiers stared at him and wondered at his stupidity, as he was already without clothes.

After that they did not let him go to his in-law's village but took him back home. They handed him to his mother after telling her what had happened. His mother started crying at the foolishness of Sheikh Chilli.

SHEIKH DRINKS TODDY

Sheikh Chilli was walking around aimlessly when he saw a man who had a rope across his shoulder with a pot attached behind. He was climbing a tree.

“What are you doing?” asked Sheikh.

“I am collecting toddy,” said the man.

“What is toddy?” asked Sheikh.

The man felt like having fun. He did not tell Sheikh that toddy was an alcoholic drink. He just said, “It is the milk of the moon. I will show you just now.”

The man climbed up the tree where there was a full pot already. He put his empty pot there and brought the full pot down.

He showed the toddy to Sheikh. It was white and Sheikh believed him that it was the milk of the moon. Sheikh said, “How does it taste?”

“Try it,” said the man.

Sheikh drank all of it and felt that it was bitter but then he started to giggle as he got drunk.

He started walking home. It took a long time for him to reach home because he didn’t seem to be able to find the way to his house.

Then he came to his house and knocked. His mother opened the door. He could not walk straight and his mother asked, "What has happened to you?"

"I have had moon milk," replied Sheikh.

"What rubbish! You have had toddy," shouted his mother.

She picked up a stick and started beating Sheikh, who promised that he would never drink toddy again.

IN PRISON

Sheikh got up in the morning with a headache. His mother started getting angry with him again.

She said, "You don't earn at all and on top of that you are getting into bad habits. You are a good for nothing son."

Sheikh felt very bad. He walked out of the house and just went on walking aimlessly.

Then he slept under a tree and woke up in the evening. He did not want to go home to hear the scolding of his mother.

So he walked away from his village. By the time he reached another village, it had become very dark.

He knew no one in that village and he had no money to go to a hotel or inn.

He was aimlessly roaming the streets when some soldiers caught him and put him in prison. He cried and shouted, but the soldiers did not let him go.

He felt miserable in the prison and after sometime he slipped out of his prison cell.

He hid behind the walls and slowly went through a side door.

Then he stopped because there was someone else there. A dacoit was standing there and he signalled to Sheikh to keep quiet.

"What are you doing here?" whispered the dacoit.

"Eh, just taking in some fresh air," hedged Sheikh.

"If you are trying to run away then I can help you," said the dacoit.

"Yes, I want to run away," admitted Sheikh.

"I have been here for five years. I have called my men and they are waiting outside. You can come with me," invited the dacoit.

From the prison building both of them ran to the outer prison wall.

Then the dacoit threw a long rope which was caught by his men, standing outside on the other side of the wall.

"Hold this rope. I will climb first then you can climb over," said the dacoit.

Sheikh nodded. He held the rope and the dacoit started climbing.

Suddenly Sheikh thought, "I am holding the rope for the dacoit. Who will hold the rope for me? How will I escape?"

So Sheikh left the rope and the dacoit lost his balance and fell down with a loud yell.

The guards came running when they heard the dacoit yell. Just as they were about to catch him, the dacoit got up and sprinted the other way, but Sheikh kept standing there.

Sheikh tried to move aside but the dacoit collided with Sheikh.

The dacoit fell on Sheikh and the guards pounced on him.

The guards thought that Sheikh had been brave and had prevented the dacoit from running away, but Sheikh knew that it had been just an accident.

Then everyone started praising Sheikh for helping in getting the dacoit caught.

Sheikh looked confused because he could not understand why everyone was praising him for being so brave.

Sheikh was then taken to the prison warden.

The warden was very happy that the dacoit had been caught and announced a reward for Sheikh Chilli.

When Sheikh pleaded that he was in the prison without having committed any crime, the warden let him free.

Sheikh quickly walked away from the prison, afraid that they might take his reward back when they come to know that he had done nothing brave.

YET ANOTHER JOB

Sheikh roamed around till he reached a friend's house in another town. The friend got him a job as a gardener.

In those days people kept horse carriages to go from one place to another.

After some days of working as a gardener, the master asked him, "Can you drive a horse carriage?"

"Yes, master," said Sheikh.

"The coachman has not come today to drive the carriage and we have to go out. You take us," ordered the master.

Sheikh did not like the rude manner in which his master was speaking, but he kept quiet and just obeyed.

The master and his wife climbed into the horse carriage. The master was in a hurry.

He said, "Let us go."

Sheikh started driving the carriage and asked, "Where do we have to go?"

Then the master said, “Go straight. I will tell you when to turn, but listen, you should not speak till I ask you something.”

“Yes, master,” nodded Sheikh and kept quiet after that.

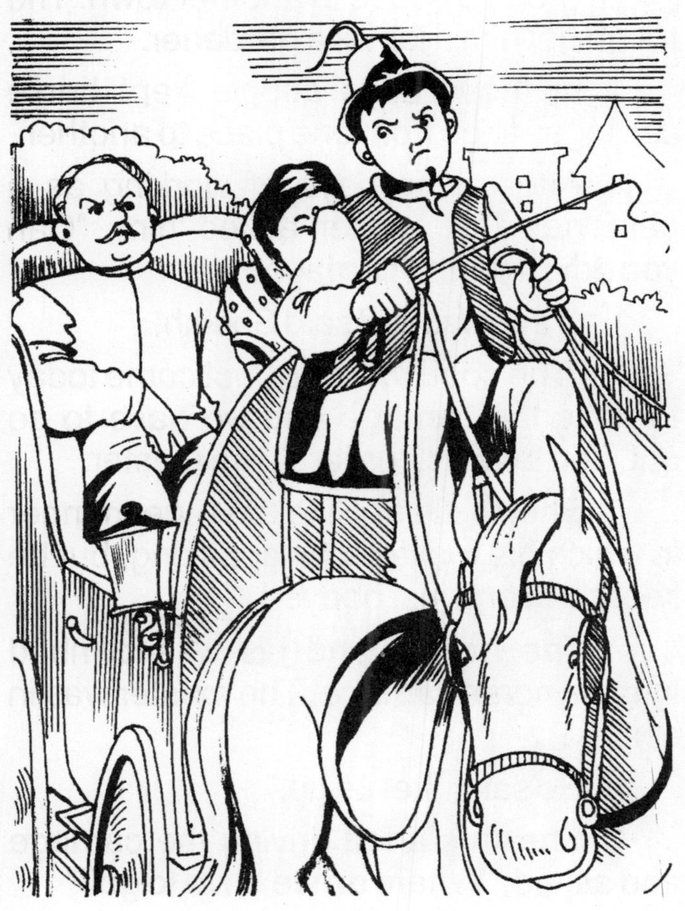

The master and his wife went for some shopping and then came back to the carriage.

As his master's wife was climbing the carriage steps, Sheikh saw her purse fall down on the road, but he did not tell them.

They had been very rude to him, so he made up his mind to teach them a lesson.

He drove on and then all of a sudden the lady screamed, "Oooh! My purse. I don't have my purse. I must have dropped it somewhere."

Sheikh kept quiet as even his master looked around for the purse.

Sheikh kept quiet as his master and his wife fought over her being so careless.

Then the master said, "Ask this stupid gardener. He might know where the purse is."

The lady asked Sheikh, "Did you see my purse?"

"Yes, I have seen it," admitted Sheikh.

"Where is it?" asked the lady.

"It fell down when you climbed into the carriage," informed her Sheikh.

"Why didn't you tell us?" she questioned.

"The master had told me to speak only when he spoke to me," said Sheikh stubbornly.

That kept them quiet. They spoke to him only once more, to order him to leave the job at once.

SHEIKH WORKS AGAIN

Sheikh Chilli tried many jobs but he was turned out from them within a few days. He returned to his mother afterwards. His mother again pestered him to start earning.

In his frustration, Sheikh swore that he would get a job by that evening.

On that day Sheikh met two school friends. He asked them if they knew of someone who could give a job to him.

They told him about a job in a house, but they said that the master treated his servants very badly.

The master would promise a good salary but he would trouble his servants so much that they left the job and when they left the job, the man would not give the servant's salary and would also snip off a bit of his ear.

He asked his friends for the direction to that house and went on his way.

Sheikh had told his mother that he would get a job by the evening, so he now decided that he would take up this job, no matter what.

He met the master and agreed to work there.

The master commanded, “You will do all the work you are told. You will get twenty rupees.”

“Yes, master,” said Sheikh meekly.

The master continued, “Your food and your stay in the house will be free but if you leave I will take one month’s salary and cut a bit of your ear to remind you that you were not a good servant.”

“What if you turn me out?” asked Sheikh.

“I never turn out servants,” answered the master.

“But if you turn me out, then I will take an year’s salary and snip off a bit of your ear,” said the Sheikh.

Nobody had spoken to the master in this way. He was shocked but then he agreed to Sheikh’s terms thinking that it could never happen.

He sent Sheikh inside the house to his wife to find out what work he had to do.

The master’s wife told him a long list of things that he had to do.

He had to clean the house, wash the utensils and clothes, go to the market and look after their small three year old son.

Sheikh did all this work but very slowly. As a result, he did not finish any work. He was always dreaming and enjoying himself.

Sheikh knew that the master could not turn him out or he would have to pay one year's salary, so he continued to work at his own sweet pace.

Soon the master's wife was fed up and wanted her husband to turn him out.

But the master replied, "I can't tell him to go, but we can make him work harder. He will either do good work or go away."

The master then called Sheikh and said, "I have a lot of land. Go there and plough it. The bullocks and the plough are with my neighbour."

"Yes, master," answered Sheikh.

The master added, "When you come back, catch a rabbit and bring some firewood."

His wife had not given Sheikh anything to eat and the master thought that after this Sheikh would leave the job.

But Sheikh had a few coins, so he ate something from the market. Then he reached the master's land.

He took the plough from the neighbour and started walking lazily behind the plough till the evening. He really enjoyed himself.

Then he remembered that he had to take firewood. The trees were far away, so he cut the plough. He could not see a rabbit, but he saw a dead dog. He dragged the dog to the master's house.

When the master saw all this, he was very angry. He told Sheikh to go inside the house and tell his wife.

His wife also became angry and thundered, "Turn this man out."

The master refused, "If I turn him out, I will have to pay an year's salary and cut my ear too. All the people will laugh at me."

"Then get me another servant," said his wife.

The master got another servant to do the housework. The master worked as a lawyer, so he took Sheikh with him everyday to keep him out of mischief.

He did not give Sheikh much to eat and he thought that in this way Sheikh would leave his job.

But Sheikh Chilli was very happy. He would sit in front of the court without any work and daydream the whole day.

When the other workers came to know that he got very little to eat, they shared their food with him, so he did not remain hungry.

In this way, Sheikh was enjoying his stay at his master's house.

He was getting paid. He had no work to do and he could sit the whole day in front of the court and daydream. He decided to never leave this job.

SHEIKH GOES TO COURT

One day, Sheikh Chilli was sitting outside the court, while the master was busy inside.

A servant came from the house and said that the master's wife wanted some money from the master to buy flour for the house.

The servant went to the courtroom to get money from his master, but the gatekeeper would not allow him inside.

The servant pleaded with the gatekeeper, but he would not listen.

The servant said to Sheikh, "If I don't take the money, the master's wife will beat me."

Sheikh told the servant not to worry. He promised that he would help him.

Then Sheikh stood at the doorway and looked inside.

He saw his master with a lot of people around him. The gatekeeper would not let him go inside.

Sheikh then shouted loudly from the gate and everybody there could hear him.

"Master, there is no money in your house and no flour. Please do something about it," Sheikh screamed at the top of his voice.

His master came out and shouted angrily, "Sheikh. Don't disturb me in the courtroom ever after this."

"Yes, master," replied Sheikh meekly.

A few days later, the same servant came running to the court where Sheikh was sitting.

He shouted, "A fire has broken out at the master's house. Tell him to come home at once."

Sheikh answered, "You go home and help in dousing the fire. I will tell the master."

As he got up to tell the master, Sheikh remembered the last incident.

He remembered how angry the master had been. He had told Sheikh not to disturb him ever again when he was in court.

So Sheikh went and sat outside the court but he did not disturb the master. When the master came out sometime later, Sheikh told him that his house was on fire.

By the time the master and Sheikh reached home, most of the house had already burnt down.

The master was again very angry but Sheikh said, "You asked me not to disturb you in the court, so I didn't."

The master had no answer.

HORSE BECOMES A HARE

The master did not have enough money to rebuild his burnt house.

His wife's father had a lot of money. So he went to his in-law's house to ask for monetary help.

He took Sheikh with him so that he would not do anything wrong at home.

On the way they reached an inn where they stayed the night. The master went inside the inn and left the hungry and sleepy Sheikh outside.

He told Sheikh, "Rub and massage the horse so that he is fresh in the morning."

Sheikh started rubbing the horse but he was very tired. Soon he fell asleep.

He woke up in the morning and when he looked around, the horse was not there.

Suddenly, in the grass nearby, he saw two ears. He held the ears and lifted them. It was a rabbit!

He held the scared rabbit high in the air. At that very time the master came out and ordered, “Bring my horse.” Sheikh pointed at the rabbit.

The angry master said, "Sheikh, bring my horse."

Sheikh Chilli kept pointing at the rabbit. His master shouted, "Sheikh, get my horse. We have to go."

Then Sheikh lifted the rabbit higher and showed it to his master again.

"I don't want a rabbit. Bring my horse," commanded the master.

Sheikh answered, "This is the horse."

The master was very very angry and shouted, "What do you mean?"

Sheikh replied, "Yesterday you told me to rub this horse."

"Yes," admitted the master.

"I rubbed the horse so much that the horse became a rabbit," said Sheikh and burst out laughing.

"Oh why did I give you this job? I am a real fool," lamented the master.

"Yes, master," agreed Sheikh, nodding his head and unable to control his laughter.

"Get lost. Leave the job. Take an year's salary and cut both my ears, but please go, Sheikh Chilli," pleaded the master.

"Keep your ears, master but give me the money," said Sheikh.

He took all the money and went back home very happy with himself.

THE GHOST

His mother was very happy that her son Sheikh Chilli had started earning money.

She was now ready to marry Sheikh to a beautiful girl named Fawzia, who was a very intelligent and nice girl. Shiekh's mother had always liked her a lot.

The wedding took place and Sheikh then went to live with his in-laws for some days.

Everyone welcomed him and looked after him. They prepared a wonderful meal for him.

After the meal, they gave him a betel leaf to eat. As he ate, the red betel juice trickled down his chin.

He saw his face in the mirror and started crying.

His wife's brother and father got very worried.

Then Sheikh said, "I am dying. See this blood coming out from my mouth."

His father-in-law burst out laughing and said, “This is not blood but the juice of betel leaves.”

Then Sheikh stopped crying.

After that his brother-in-law took Sheikh out to show him around the city. They came back in the evening feeling very tired.

Sheikh lay down and he was so tired that he slept at once, but a mosquito started troubling him.

He went on hitting at the mosquito but it came buzzing near him again and again.

Then Sheikh picked his slipper and hit the mosquito but the mosquito flew away.

The slipper hit the pot of honey that was tied above the bed. Sheikh went back to sleep unaware of it.

The honey started dripping and falling on the sleeping Sheikh. He dreamt that he was eating honey in a beautiful garden.

But all of a sudden he felt very sticky. He woke up and found himself soaked in honey.

He felt that he must have a bath and wash off the honey.

So he decided to go to the river to take a bath.

He opened the door of the room and started looking for the way out. He reached the storeroom and fell on a pile of cottonwool that was kept to make quilts.

Just then his sister-in-law saw him. She shouted, "Ghost! Ghost!"

Sheikh went towards her to calm her. When she saw the 'ghost' coming towards her, she ran outside, shouting, "Ghost! Ghost! Help!"

Sheikh quickly ran out of the main door towards the river. On the way was a sheep pen. He tripped and fell down.

Suddenly he felt someone move behind him and say, "This sheep is the biggest. I must steal this one."

Sheikh realised that the man was a thief. He felt very afraid and he tried to move away from the thief. The thief saw him move.

Then the thief threw a blanket on Sheikh thinking that he was a sheep and picked him up.

Sheikh shouted, "What are you doing? Where are you taking me? Stop it. Leave me."

The thief screamed, "A talking sheep!"

He threw Sheikh on the ground and ran away because he was frightened. He thought that it was not a sheep but a ghost!

The thief even left behind the blanket he had brought along to steal the sheep.

Sheikh ran to the river and cleaned off the cottonwool and the honey from his body and head.

Then he wrapped the blanket around him and walked to his in-law's house. He met his brother-in-law who was looking very worried.

The brother-in-law asked, "Where were you? There is a ghost inside the storeroom."

"Don't worry, I will tackle the ghost," replied Sheikh bravely.

He opened the door of the storeroom and went in, locking it from inside.

Sheikh knew there was no ghost there. Pretending to be brave, Sheikh shouted, "I will not spare you, Mr. ghost."

Sheikh then started to beat the stick all around the room, pretending to beat the ghost.

He continued shouting in a loud voice, "You better leave this house and go or I will kill you. Dare not come back ever."

After some time Sheikh came out and declared, "Now there is nothing to worry. The ghost has gone. All of you can relax."

Everyone praised Sheikh for his courage. They were glad to have such a brave man for their son-in-law.

THE HOLY THREAD

Sheikh Chilli went to cut wood one day from the forest. He felt happy to be there because the weather was very pleasant.

Then he sat on a branch and started cutting it.

He didn't realise that he was cutting the same branch on which he was sitting.

He started daydreaming as he was cutting. Then he saw some ants going past in a row.

He started thinking that the ants were going to their king and the king would come wearing a crown.

The king would then talk to Sheikh and look after him and he would have a wonderful time.

Just then a man shouted, "Be careful or you will fall."

Sheikh Chilli turned around to the man standing below and said, "What did you say?"

"Be careful. You are cutting the branch on which you are sitting. You will fall," said the man.

Just then the branch broke and Sheikh Chilli fell, but he was lucky.

He did not get hurt because he fell on a heap of leaves.

Sheikh got up and asked that man, "How did you know that I was going to fall? Can you tell about the future?"

"Yes, of course," said the man cunningly.

He was telling a lie. He was a tailor and did not know how to read the future at all.

He had understood that Sheikh was a fool and so he wanted to make some quick money.

Sheikh walked to him and requested, "Please tell me about my future."

"You will have to give me one rupee for it," demanded the tailor.

"I have one anna. It is less than a rupee so just tell me how long will I live," Sheikh asked the tailor.

The tailor said, "Death is right behind you. You will not live very long. No one can save you from an early death."

Sheikh felt very afraid but felt relieved when the tailor said, "I am giving you a holy thread. Till you keep wearing it, you will not die."

The tailor took out a black thread that he had and tied it around the neck of Sheikh's neck.

Sheikh came home and told his wife Fawzia. She burst out laughing and removed the thread from around his neck.

She declared, "That man has fooled you. He did all this just to take your money."

Sheikh lay down on the floor. Fawzia asked, "What is the matter?"

Sheikh lamented, "You have cut the black thread which was the thread of my life. Now I am dead."

Just then his mother came in and got alarmed to see Sheikh lying on the floor.

Fawzia told her what had happened.

Sheikh repeated, "I am dead. I am not on earth."

His mother shouted, "No, you are not dead. You are on earth in your own house."

But Sheikh refused to believe it. He kept lying on the floor saying, "I am dead."

Then his wife interrupted him naughtily, "Mother, your son says he is dead. Now he cannot eat the sweets you have bought. Give them to me. I will throw them into the dustbin."

At once Sheikh got up because he loved sweets. He exclaimed, “No! Don’t throw the sweets. I have come back to life.”

Fawzia and Sheikh Chilli’s mother had a good laugh.

AS A GUEST

Sheikh's wife Fawzia was very worried. She told Sheikh, "Both Mother and I are going away. I don't think we should leave you alone in the house."

"I can look after myself," asserted Sheikh.

"Last time you nearly put the house on fire when you were alone," reminded Fawzia.

"Don't worry. This time I plan to go to visit my cousin Irfan," declared Sheikh.

"That is a nice idea. But you must only return a day after we return," said Fawzia.

"That is no problem. Irfan often used to stay with us for a long time. I can stay there for a month," answered Sheikh Chilli.

So Sheikh went to his cousin Irfan's house who lived with his wife and two children.

Irfan was very happy to see Sheikh but his wife was not so pleased.

For the first week she was quiet but after that she wanted Sheikh to go away.

So one evening when Irfan returned with Sheikh from the shop, she told them that she had to go as her father was sick.

Irfan said, "I think we four should go to see him. What will you do Sheikh?"

Sheikh answered, "I hope your father gets well soon. You don't worry about the house. I will look after it. I will stay here."

Irfan's wife interrupted him, "But how will you stay here as there is nothing to eat in the house? I had locked the kitchen and now I can't find the keys."

Sheikh could not dream of staying without eating, so he replied, "Then tomorrow morning I will go away. In the night I will think about which neighbour's house I should go to."

Irfan's wife had actually hidden the key of the kitchen in her room.

The family went away and Sheikh was to leave the next morning. But Sheikh was very hungry the next morning. He decided to look for the missing keys.

In the meantime when Irfan reached his in-law's house and found that his father-in-law was well, he got angry with his wife for telling a lie.

Next morning he made his family return home.

They came back to see that Sheikh was still there. Sheikh welcomed them and told them that he had not gone because he had found the kitchen keys and now he could cook plenty of food to eat. Irfan's wife was dismayed.

Sheikh continued staying with them.

For a week, Irfan's wife kept quiet, but Sheikh did not go back to his house.

Then one day she started groaning and shouting that she had a stomach ache.

She told Sheikh, "This pain is like the pain you told me your mother had. Can you get me the medicine from your village?"

"Yes, I will get you the medicine," replied Sheikh at once.

Irfan's wife apologised, "I am sorry for giving you this trouble. Your house is so far away."

"That doesn't matter. I will bring the medicine," said Sheikh.

She refused, "No. You live so far away. It will be too much for you. So you tell the doctor to give the medicine and I will send someone to fetch it."

Sheikh said, "I will go in the morning because in the night I might lose my way."

But in the night Sheikh had a bad dream.

Sheikh dreamt that a lion was chasing him. As he tried to save himself, he fell off his bed.

In the morning Irfan came and saw that Sheikh was not there. He shouted to his wife, “Sheikh has gone.” His wife came running happily.

Irfan said, “It seems that Sheikh went away early in the morning.”

“That is really wonderful,” yelled his wife jubilantly.

“See how much he cares for you. He has gone for your medicine,” Irfan pointed out.

“I told him not to come back because his village is so far,” she said.

“Then how will you get your medicine?” asked Irfan.

“I don’t need the medicine,” she replied.

“But you had a stomach ache,” interrupted Irfan.

“I am not sick,” she declared.

Sheikh got up suddenly from under the bed and spoke up. “And I haven’t really gone.”

“What!” exclaimed Irfan’s wife.

“It is good that I didn’t go this morning as you are not sick. Now can I have my breakfast please?” asked Sheikh.

Irfan's wife could not say anything. She just looked at Sheikh and nodded her head wordlessly.

Then helplessly, she burst out crying as Sheikh added, "Please I need to have a heavy breakfast as I am very hungry."

SHEIKH HUNTS A TIGER

Sheikh got a job in the court of a king who ruled a small kingdom. Sheikh was now thought to be a very respectable person.

One day the king was going to the forest to hunt.

Sheikh suggested, "I want to come with you, My Lord."

"What will you do there, Sheikh?" asked the king.

"I want a chance to show you how good I am at hunting," said Sheikh.

Hunting in those days was done by sitting on wooden platforms made on the trees and waiting for the tiger to come. They would tie a goat below so that the tiger would come to eat it.

Sheikh accompanied the king to the forest.

The king and his nobles sat on one tree platform and Sheikh sat with another courtier on the other 'machaan' as they were called.

Sheikh did not like it. He cribbed, "What kind of hunting is this? We are sitting and waiting for the poor animal. We should be going like an army with our guns straight, looking the tiger in the eye. There he comes. He is looking at me and I am looking at him."

He continued dreamily, “I am not afraid at all and I will kill him and the world will praise me for being a very brave man.”

While he was talking, a real tiger had walked up to eat the goat but Sheikh was not aware of it.

Deep in his dreams, he said, "There you tiger, now I will finish you." Dhhhaaaam.

The gun roared. Sheikh had actually pressed the trigger without knowing it. The bullet hit the tiger, who died. The others did not know that Sheikh had fired the shot accidently while dreaming.

The courtier with him praised him, "That was wonderful Sheikh. You hit the tiger."

The king came and applauded, "I thought that I was good at hunting but you, Sheikh are better than me. That was a wonderful shot."

Sheikh looked confused for he could not believe that he had killed the tiger. When Sheikh realised that he had actually killed a tiger, he enjoyed everyone's praise. The king rewarded Sheikh Chilli but Sheikh never understood how he had killed the tiger.

ANOTHER THIEF

Sheikh was not worried at all when everyone kept talking that in the kingdom there was a thief who was looting everyone.

Sheikh had earned good money but he spent so much that he had little left with him.

So he was not afraid that any thief would come to rob him because there was nothing with him worth robbing.

One night, Sheikh started feeling uneasy. He went to the terrace to walk a little before he slept.

As he walked, he started thinking about his parents. His father had died a long time back and his mother too had died.

He remembered how loving his mother had been. His carefree childhood days came back to him.

His eyes filled with tears as he thought of her.

Then he started thinking of something he had loved doing during his childhood.

He had loved flying kites and now he started dreaming that he was flying a kite and he was shouting to the kite, “Go up, up and up.”

And Sheikh fell down from the terrace. While dreaming he fell over the terrace parapet, onto the ground, right on top of a thief. The thief screamed, “Oooooh!”

Sheikh did not know that the man was a thief. He got up quickly because he could feel that a man was under him who was screaming, "Oh! I am hurt very badly."

Sheikh asked the man on whom he had fallen, "Where are you hurt? Tell me."

As soon as he heard someone speaking, the man remembered that he was a thief. He started running to escape from Sheikh.

Just then the neighbours came over because they had heard Sheikh screaming.

When they saw a man running away from Sheikh, they caught him.

Then they took the man to the court and found that he was the thief who was responsible for so many robberies.

Everyone praised Sheikh for catching the thief. A neighbour took Sheikh to the king and said, "My Lord, Sheikh Chilli is so brave that he jumped from the terrace to catch this thief."

The king praised his courage, “Well done Sheikh! From today onwards your full expenses will be borne by me.”

Sheikh was really happy as just falling from the terrace had solved all his money problems.

THE WINNING LIE

The king liked Sheikh because he found him very simple, but his son, the prince, did not like him at all.

One day the prince declared that he would have a competition to find out who could tell the biggest lie.

Many people came and told lies but the prince would say, "This is not a lie. This can happen."

One person lied, "I have seen ants as big as elephants."

Another quipped, "I have a watermelon plant growing inside me because I ate the seeds of a watermelon."

"But that could happen, so that is not a lie," denied the prince.

When all the liars had been sent away, Sheikh Chilli requested, "May I speak, My Lord?"

"Yes, you may. So what does your little brain say?" asked the prince.

"It says that you are the biggest fool and you should not be made the king," declared Sheikh loudly and firmly.

Everyone was shocked. The prince shouted, "Arrest Sheikh."

Then Sheikh said, "My Lord, you wanted to hear a lie and this is the biggest lie." Now the prince could not say anything to Sheikh.

Everyone started laughing and the prize money was given to Sheikh Chilli.

ON A TRAIN AGAIN

Sheikh had been on a train when he was four years old but he did not remember the journey. After that he had never been on a train.

Once he had to go to another city and he thought that he would go by train. In those days, trains had three types of ticket fares–the first class, the second class and the cheapest was the third class.

Sheikh reached the station but did not know what to do. He asked a man who told him that he should buy a ticket first.

Sheikh asked, "What does the train look like?"

The man said, "It is big and black in colour and smoke comes out from it."

Sheikh went to buy a ticket for Delhi. He asked for a ticket and the man repiled, "Give me five rupees."

Sheikh shouted, "That is too much. Take less money."

"Does this train belong to your father-in-law that you can pay less than the ticket fare?" replied the man angrily.

Just as Sheikh bought the ticket, he saw a big and tall ticket checker wearing a black coat and smoke was coming out from his cigarette. Sheikh ran and climbed onto his back.

"What are you doing?" shouted the ticket checker.

"Come on, train. Take me to Delhi station," yelled Sheikh jumping up and down on his back.

The ticket checker got very angry and made Sheikh get off his back with the help of other people. Then Sheikh was led to his train.

After that Sheikh sat in the train and as the train started moving, he began to enjoy himself watching the beautiful scenery outside.

But then another ticket checker came. He asked for his train ticket.

Sheikh gave him his ticket and the checker said, "You will have to pay more money."

"Why?" asked Sheikh.

"You are sitting in the first class but your ticket is for the third class," explained the ticket checker.

"What is the difference between them that you are charging so much extra money?" asked Sheikh.

"The first class seats have cushions but the third class bogie seats are wooden benches," said the ticket checker.

Sheikh stood up and declared, "I don't need cushions."

Then he tore away the cushions from the seat.

Sheikh said, “I have taken out the cushions. Now I can sit here in the first class with the same third class ticket.”

But the ticket checker would not agree. He told Sheikh that he would either have to go to the third class compartment of the train or pay more to sit in the first class.

Sheikh said loudly, “I will not pay any more money.”

The ticket checker shouted, “You have damaged the seat. You will also have to pay damages.”

“What cheats you all are! First you take so much money for the ticket and then you don’t let us sit where we want. I will not give a single paisa,” yelled Sheikh.

As soon as the train slowed down, a passenger informed them, “I think the next station is coming.”

The ticket checker waited for the train to stop. Then he called the railway police and told them about Sheikh.

The policemen took Sheikh out of the first class and made him sit in the third class.

THE QUTUB MINAR

In Delhi, Sheikh went to see the Qutub Minar.

All the people standing there were looking up to see the very tall pillar like tower.

A man told them that King Qutbuddin had made this very tall tower called Qutub Minar.

It was made so that a priest could go on top of the building and shout out to the people of Delhi that it was time for prayers which they called 'aazaan'.

One person looking at the tall tower of the Qutub Minar wondered, "There were no cranes and machines. Then how did they construct this building?"

Another man started joking and said, "The people then must have been huge giants, so they made this tall tower easily. The giants would have carried the pillars and placed them one on the other. They must have built the minar this way."

A third man laughed and joined in the fun, saying, "I think I know. They must have made the Qutub Minar flat on the ground and then straightened it."

But then Sheikh said very seriously, "I know how it was made. They must have dug a deep well and then turned it upside down." All the people burst out laughing at his stupidity.

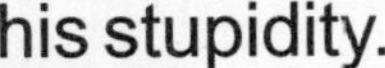

THE TAJ MAHAL

Sheikh went to Agra to see the Taj Mahal. He loved the white marble monument.

Some people told him that the Taj Mahal was ordered to be made by Emperor Shahjahan in memory of his beautiful wife Mumtaz Mahal.

It had a dome in the middle and four towers on the corners. The River Yamuna flowed behind it.

Sheikh went inside the lovely monument and saw the wonderful hall, full of people who had come to see the Taj Mahal. He saw the two graves of the Emperor Shahjahan and the Empress Mumtaz Mahal.

He walked around for some more time and then feeling tired he sat down to relax in the beautiful lawns in front of the Taj Mahal.

Nearby, two drunk men were talking and Sheikh Chilli overheard their conversation.

One drunk said, “I can give only twenty thousand rupees for the Taj Mahal. Not a rupee more because it is such an old building.”

“But I am ready to pay even thirty thousand rupees. It is old but beautiful,” replied the other.

Thinking that Taj Mahal was really up for sale and wanting to buy it for himself, Sheikh decided to trick the drunk men.

Sheikh walked up to them and pretending to know nothing about their quarrel, he asked them, "Why are you two fighting? Can I be of any help?"

The drunk men repeated their quarrel in front of Sheikh and told him to decide who should buy the Taj.

Sheikh said, "But none of you can actually buy the Taj Mahal because I am not ready to sell it. I own it."

Feeling pleased with his intelligence, Sheikh walked away. He heard the first drunk say, "So he is the owner of the Tajmahal."

The other said, "You talked so loudly that is why the owner heard us."

"Yes, what a big loss we both have suffered by not being able to buy the Taj Mahal," said the first man.

Sheikh laughed at their foolishness and began looking for the person who owned the Taj so that he could buy it from him!